The Role of Immigrants in the U.S. Labor Market

Introduction and Summary

The role of immigrants in the U.S. labor market has long generated substantial interest among policymakers. Lawmakers have considered a broad range of issues concerning foreign-born workers, from the number of immigrants permitted to enter the United States and the criteria for determining who is admitted to the rules governing their employment and myriad questions related to undocumented workers.[1] Bills introduced in the 109th Congress, for example, would alter the laws governing the admission of temporary workers under the H-2A program for agricultural workers and the H-2B program for other workers; change the requirements for gaining permanent admission to the United States; and take steps to reduce illegal immigration. President George W. Bush has called for a new temporary guest worker program that would provide temporary legal status to certain foreign-born workers who are working in the United States without authorization.

The United States is known as a nation of immigrants—a characterization that is more appropriate today than at any time since the 1930s. Census Bureau data for 2004 indicate that 34 million of the nation's 288 million people—12 percent of the U.S. population—were foreign born. That was the highest percentage of foreign-born people the Census Bureau had recorded in 70 years.

People immigrate to the United States for many reasons: to join family members, to seek better economic opportunities, to escape persecution, or simply to get a fresh start. The presence of so many people from other countries necessarily has important consequences for U.S. society. This paper concentrates on one aspect of their presence that is of particular importance for the nation's economy: their role in the U.S. labor market.

Foreign-Born Workers

Immigrants are a substantial and growing segment of the U.S. labor force. In 2004, more than 21 million workers—one in seven workers in the United States—were foreign born, and half had arrived since 1990. Almost 40 percent of foreign-born workers were from Mexico and Central America, and 25 percent were from Asia.[2]

To a considerable extent, educational attainment determines the role of immigrants in the labor market. Even as the number of native-born workers without a high school diploma is shrinking, the number of foreign-born workers without a diploma continues to increase. In 2004, among workers age 25 and older who lacked a diploma, nearly half were foreign born, and most were from Mexico and Central America. At the same time, many other immigrant groups were highly educated. The educational attainment of foreign-born workers from other regions was slightly higher than that of natives; in particular, a higher percentage of those immigrants had taken graduate courses.

Many workers from Mexico and Central America were employed in jobs that required little formal education. Workers from that region earned much less, on average, than did the typical native worker. In 2004, three-quarters of workers born in Mexico and Central America were employed in occupations that have minimal educational requirements, such as construction laborer and dishwasher; only one-quarter of native workers held such jobs. On average, the weekly earnings of men from Mexico and Central America who worked full time were about half those of native-born men; women from Mexico and Central America earned about three-fifths of the average weekly earnings of native-born women.

---

1. The terms "immigrant" and "foreign born" are used interchangeably throughout this paper.

2. For a general description of the foreign-born population, see Congressional Budget Office, *A Description of the Immigrant Population* (November 2004).

Other foreign-born workers—that is, those who immigrated to the United States from places other than Mexico and Central America—were employed in a much broader range of occupations. A notable exception is their concentration in fields such as computer and mathematical sciences, which generally require at least a college education. For workers from the rest of the world, the average weekly earnings of men and women were similar to those of native-born men and women.

Impact on the Labor Market

The arrival of large numbers of immigrants with little education probably slows the growth of the wages of native-born high school dropouts, at least initially, but the ultimate impact on wages is difficult to quantify. Recent estimates of the effect of two decades of growth in the foreign-born workforce on the average earnings of native high school dropouts have ranged from negligible to an earnings reduction of almost 10 percent. The wide range of those estimates reflects, in part, the uncertainty surrounding what employers and native workers would have done if those foreign-born workers had not been present, either initially or after employers and workers had adjusted to the changes in opportunities that the influx of immigrants produced.

A flexible labor market will adjust over time to the presence of more foreign-born workers. The U.S. economy should attract more capital as investors see opportunities to increase their returns. Increased investment, in turn, will tend to raise workers' productivity and earnings. Ultimately, lower production costs should increase employers' profits and lower prices for consumers. Even after such adjustments occur, however, the earnings of native workers whose education and skills are most like those of immigrants could be adversely affected by the increased competition. Over even longer time periods, some of those workers may be motivated to obtain additional education to receive the increased labor market payoffs associated with greater education.

Implications for the Future

Immigrants have been—and in all likelihood will continue to be—a major source of new workers in the United States. Barring substantial shifts in demographic trends, immigrants and their descendants are expected to provide the majority of the nation's population growth during the next half century. Who immigrates to the United States and what those immigrants and their descendants do

after their arrival will increasingly determine the size and skill composition of the U.S. labor force.

Foreign-Born Workers

Although immigrant workers can be found in virtually every industry and occupation, they are concentrated in certain low-skill sectors. This is particularly true of recent immigrants from Mexico and Central America.

This section examines the growth and characteristics of the foreign-born workforce and then focuses on their labor market outcomes, especially their earnings. Their lower earnings reflect, at least in part, the fact that many of them have less to offer potential employers than do native-born workers. On average, they have fewer years of education and experience. Many of them do not speak English very well, if at all.[3] And, at least initially, they may not be familiar with how things are done in the U.S. labor market.

Growth in the Foreign-Born Labor Force

The growth of the economy derives from capital accumulation, productivity increases, and the growth of the labor force. During the past decade, foreign-born workers accounted for more than half of the growth of the U.S. labor force. The number of foreign-born workers increased from 13 million in 1994 to 21 million in 2004 (see Table 1).

Foreign-born workers include those who are naturalized U.S. citizens, those who are not citizens but are authorized immigrants, and those who are unauthorized immigrants. About 40 percent of foreign-born workers are U.S. citizens. Possibly half (6 million to 7 million) of the remaining foreign-born workers are unauthorized (see Box 1 on page 4).

In 2004, almost 40 percent of foreign-born workers were from Mexico and Central America (see Table 2 on page 6). Another 25 percent were from Asia, including the Philippines, India, China, Vietnam, and Korea. Most of the remaining foreign-born workers had come from other parts of the Western Hemisphere and Europe.

---

3.   In the 2000 census, 25 million of the 31 million foreign-born people age 5 and older residing in the United States indicated that they spoke a language other than English at home, including about 9 million who indicated that they did not speak English very well or at all.

Table 1.

Size and Growth of the U.S. Labor Force Age 16 and Older, by Nativity, 1994 and 2004

| | Number (Millions) | | Growth, 1994 to 2004 | |
	1994	2004	In Millions	Percentage Change
Total	131.1	147.4	16.3	12
Native Born	118.1	126.0	7.8	7
Foreign Born	12.9	21.4	8.5	66
Mexico and Central America	4.6	8.3	3.7	80
Rest of world	8.3	13.1	4.8	58

Source: Congressional Budget Cffice based on the Bureau of the Census, Current Population Surveys, 1994 and 2004.

Sharp differences exist between the educational attainment of workers from Mexico and Central America and that of workers from other parts of the world, as shown in Table 2. Workers from Mexico and Central America typically had completed about nine years of education. Workers from other countries had completed an average of 14 years of education, which was slightly higher than the average educational attainment of native-born workers.[4] Those differences are important because the education and skills that foreign-born workers bring to the job largely determine the impact those workers have on the U.S. labor market.

The differences in educational attainment by country of origin appear to reflect the basis on which foreign-born workers were admitted to the United States, rather than differences in educational levels in their home country. For example, the average educational attainment of workers who came from India was 16 years, even though the average educational attainment of the adult population in India is well below high school level. Many workers from India were admitted to the United States because they had skills that were in demand.[5]

Although immigrants work in every part of the country, two-thirds of them reside in just six states, where only one-third of native-born workers live. The foreign born constitute 32 percent of the labor force in California and average 21 percent of the labor force in Florida, Illinois,

New Jersey, New York, and Texas, compared with an average of only 8 percent in the remaining 44 states (see Table 3 on page 7).

During the past decade, the share of workers who are foreign born has been growing in the rest of the country by almost as much as it has in the six largest immigrant-receiving states. The share of the labor force that is foreign born increased 4.2 percentage points in those 44 states, compared with 4.7 percentage points in California and 5.6 percentage points in the five other large immigrant-receiving states.

California and New York are not only major gateways for new immigrants but also major sources of foreign-born workers for other states. Internal migration has recently had a substantial effect on the growth of the foreign-born population of states such as Arkansas, Georgia, Nevada, and North Carolina. The foreign-born population of some of those states also grew significantly as a result of direct migration from abroad.[6]

Over half of all foreign-born workers live in seven consolidated metropolitan areas where only a fifth of native-

---

4. Average educational attainment is based on an estimate of the highest grade of formal school attended and completed for each person in the group. Thus, someone who completed 11 years of school and later obtained a credential based on passing the General Educational Development tests (GED) would be classified for this purpose as having 11 years of education.

5. Information from the Office of Immigration Statistics indicates that 40 percent of the immigrants from India who came to the United States in fiscal year 2003 were admitted on an employment-based preference, whereas only 3 percent of immigrants from Mexico and Central America were admitted on that basis. See Department of Homeland Security, Office of Immigration Statistics, *2003 Yearbook of Immigration Statistics* (September 2004), pp. 29-32.

6. Marc J. Perry and Jason P. Schachter, *Migration of Natives and the Foreign Born: 1995 to 2000*, Census 2000 Special Reports (Bureau of the Census, August 2003), p. 5, available at www.census.gov/prod/2003pubs/censr-11.pdf.

Box 1.
Measuring the Number of Unauthorized Immigrants

Considerable uncertainty is inherent in estimates of the number of unauthorized immigrants that reside in the United States and the number that are in the labor force. The decennial census, the Current Population Survey (CPS), and similar sources of information about the population and labor force do not ask foreign-born people about their legal status in the United States aside from whether they are naturalized citizens. Thus, the number of unauthorized immigrants must be estimated by indirect methods that introduce the possibility of significant errors. A recent analysis, based on survey data from the CPS and administrative data from the Department of Homeland Security and other federal agencies, indicated that in early 2004 about 10 million foreign-born people were living in the United States without authorization and about 6.3 million of them were in the labor force.

Population Estimates
The methodology used in recent estimates of the unauthorized foreign-born population subtracts the estimated number of legal immigrants from the estimated total number of immigrants. Those two quantities are developed from different data sources and estimates of several factors for which definitive information is not available.

Estimates of the total number of immigrants are usually based on the number of foreign-born people in a census or survey. That number is then adjusted upward for the population missed or not covered by the survey and adjusted downward for the population that is in the United States temporarily, such as foreign students and diplomats. The number of legal immigrants is estimated from the number of green cards, which confer permanent legal resident status, that the government has issued over a period; that number is adjusted for emigration and death, for which little definitive information is available. Refugee arrivals and asylum approvals are included in the legal immigrant population in the year those immi-grants arrive or obtain approval, not when they obtain green cards.

Two estimates of the unauthorized foreign-born population in 2000 illustrate their sensitivity to the methods used to produce them. Both estimates were significantly larger than earlier estimates because they were based on the 2000 census, which counted many more immigrants than previous surveys had found.[1] The larger estimate of 8.3 million, produced by Jeffrey Passel and his colleagues, began with the number of foreign-born people who came to the United States since 1980 and subtracted the estimated number residing in the United States legally in 2000. The smaller estimate of 7.0 million, produced by Robert Warren, began with an estimate of the unauthorized immigrant population for 1990 and updated it using information from the 2000 census and other sources.

In a more recent estimate, Passel puts the size of the unauthorized foreign-born population at 10.3 million in 2004.[2] That figure is derived from an estimated foreign-born population of 35.7 million in March 2004, from which were subtracted 10.4 million legal permanent residents, 11.3 million naturalized citizens, 1.2 million temporary legal residents,

---

1. Jeffrey S. Passel, Jennifer Van Hook, and Frank D. Bean, *Estimates of the Legal and Unauthorized Foreign-Born Population for the United States and Selected States, Based on Census 2000* (report submitted by the Urban Institute to the Bureau of the Census, June 2004); Robert Warren, *Estimates of the Unauthorized Immigrant Population Residing in the United States, 1990 to 2000* (U.S. Immigration and Naturalization Service, January 2003), available at http://uscis.gov/graphics/shared/aboutus/statistics/Ill_Report_1211.pdf

2. Jeffrey S. Passel, "Unauthorized Migrants: Numbers and Characteristics" (background briefing prepared for the Task Force on Immigration and America's Future, Pew Hispanic Center, June 14, 2005). In this and earlier reports, Passel and his coauthors have provided the most comprehensive estimates of the unauthorized foreign-born population available.

Box 1.

Continued

and 2.5 million refugee arrivals.[1] Note that between 1 million and 1.5 million people who have employment authorization documents of other types were not subtracted and therefore were included in the population of unauthorized immigrants.[2]

Labor Force Estimates

Far fewer studies have attempted to estimate the number of unauthorized immigrants in the labor force. Jeffrey Passel provided the most recent estimate.[3] He calculated that about 6.3 million of the 10.3 unauthorized immigrants in the United States in March 2004 were in the labor force. That estimate suggests that about 30 percent of all foreign-born workers were unauthorized immigrants.

Passel's methodology for estimating the number of unauthorized immigrants in the labor force is quite different from the one he used to estimate the size of the unauthorized immigrant population. For his

labor force estimate, Passel applied a procedure that assigns an immigration status to each foreign-born individual in the Current Population Survey; the assignment of status is based on information about individuals available in that survey, as well as other information about people who receive various types of visas or who are unauthorized. Once the immigration status is designated, it is a straightforward process to tabulate the number of people with a particular immigration status, such as undocumented immigrant, and the number with a particular labor force status, such as employed or unemployed.

Most assignments were based on a person's satisfying a particular set of criteria. For example, a person who was the spouse or child of a U.S. citizen was assigned the status of legal permanent resident. A person from a particular country who came to the United States during a period of influx of refugees from that country was assigned the status of refugee.

Designating the status of unauthorized immigrant was more complex. That status was assigned probabilistically based on an individual's characteristics, including occupation, country of origin, age, and sex, and the estimated fraction of people with those characteristics who were unauthorized migrants. That fraction was estimated using a special survey of formerly unauthorized immigrants at the time they acquired legal status under the Immigration Reform and Control Act of 1986. For example, food service and household workers had a high probability of being undocumented, whereas judges had a zero probability. Any remaining foreign-born people in the survey who were not assigned a status through any of the tests were assumed to be legal permanent residents.

---

1. The estimate of 35.7 million for the foreign-born population differs from the estimate of 34 million foreign-born people cited in the text because the former figure includes adjustments for the foreign-born population in the military and living in institutions, as well as an estimate by Passel and his colleagues of an undercount of the foreign-born population in the 2000 census.

2. For example, persons with temporary protected status and extended voluntary departure status and those who have applied for those statuses may account for 3 percent to 4 percent of the unauthorized immigrant population. Also, more than 6 percent of the unauthorized migrant population have applied for green cards but are waiting for them to be issued. In total, between 10 percent and 15 percent of unauthorized immigrants are known to the Department of Homeland Security and have their full legal status pending.

3. Passel, "Unauthorized Migrants: Numbers and Characteristics."

Table 2.

Composition and Educational Attainment of the U.S. Labor Force Age 16 and Older, by Nativity, 2004

	Number (Millions)	Percentage of Labor Force	Percentage of Foreign-Born Labor Force	Average Years of Education Completed
Labor Force Age 16 and Older	147.4	100.0	n.a.	13.5
Native born	126.0	85.5	n.a.	13.7
Foreign born	21.4	14.5	100.0	12.2
Mexico and Central America	8.3	5.7	39.0	9.4
Mexico	6.6	4.5	30.7	9.3
El Salvador	0.7	0.5	3.3	9.2
Guatemala	0.4	0.2	1.7	8.8
Honduras	0.3	0.2	1.2	9.7
Nicaragua, Panama, Costa Rica, Belize, other Central America	0.4	0.3	2.0	11.5
Rest of World	13.1	8.9	61.0	14.0
Asia	5.4	3.7	25.4	14.6
Philippines	0.9	0.6	4.4	14.6
India	0.9	0.6	4.0	16.1
China	0.7	0.5	3.4	14.6
Vietnam	0.6	0.4	2.9	12.8
Korea	0.4	0.3	2.0	14.7
Other Asia	1.9	1.3	8.7	14.5
Europe and Canada	2.8	1.9	13.0	14.4
Canada	0.4	0.3	1.8	14.8
England	0.3	0.2	1.3	15.1
Poland	0.3	0.2	1.3	13.9
Other Europe	1.9	1.3	8.6	14.3
Caribbean	2.2	1.5	10.1	12.7
Cuba	0.6	0.4	2.6	13.0
Dominican Republic	0.4	0.3	2.1	12.0
Jamaica	0.4	0.3	2.1	13.2
Haiti	0.4	0.3	1.8	12.5
Other Caribbean	0.3	0.2	1.5	13.2
South America	1.4	0.9	6.5	13.2
Colombia	0.3	0.2	1.5	13.3
Other South America	1.1	0.7	5.0	13.2
Other Regions	1.4	0.9	6.5	13.2
Africa	0.3	0.2	1.5	13.3
Oceana	1.1	0.7	5.0	13.2
Other unspecified	1.3	0.9	6.0	13.6

Source: Congressional Budget Office based on the Bureau of the Census, Current Population Surveys, 2004.

Note: n.a. = not applicable.

Table 3.

Geographic Distribution of Native- and Foreign-Born Workers, 1994 and 2004

| | Number (Millions) | | | | Percentage of the Labor Force | | | |
	Calif.	N.Y., Fla., Tex., N.J., and Ill.	Rest of Country	Total	Calif.	N.Y., Fla., Tex., N.J., and Ill.	Rest of Country	Total
				Distribution in 2004				
Total	17.6	39.5	90.3	147.4	100.0	100.0	100.0	100.0
Native Born	11.9	31.3	82.8	126.0	67.7	79.2	91.7	85.5
Foreign Born	5.7	8.2	7.5	21.4	32.3	20.8	8.3	14.5
Mexico and Central America	3.0	2.7	2.7	8.3	17.0	6.8	3.0	5.7
Rest of world	2.7	5.5	4.8	13.1	15.3	14.0	5.4	8.9
				Distribution in 1994				
Total	15.5	34.8	80.7	131.1	100.0	100.0	100.0	100.0
Native Born	11.2	29.5	77.4	118.1	72.5	84.8	95.8	90.1
Foreign Born	4.3	5.3	3.4	12.9	27.5	15.2	4.2	9.9
Mexico and Central America	2.5	1.5	0.6	4.6	16.0	4.3	0.8	3.5
Rest of world	1.8	3.8	2.7	8.3	11.5	10.8	3.4	6.3

Source: Congressional Budget Office based on the Bureau of the Census, Current Population Surveys, 1994 and 2004.

born workers live. Foreign-born workers are most concentrated in Miami, Florida, where 60 percent of the workforce is foreign born. In 16 of the 242 metropolitan areas throughout the United States, foreign-born workers constitute more than 30 percent of the workforce. The greatest number of foreign-born workers—more than 3.2 million—live in California in the Los Angeles/Long Beach/Riverside/San Bernardino consolidated metropolitan area, where they represent 16 percent of foreign-born workers nationwide. Native-born workers in that area, by contrast, represent only 4 percent of the national total of native workers. Foreign-born workers are much more likely than native-born workers to live in central cities (43 percent of foreign-born workers versus 25 percent of natives) and much less likely to be in nonmetropolitan areas (6 percent versus 23 percent).

What the Foreign Born Bring to the Labor Market

The foreign born have diverse characteristics that are important to the labor market, especially the amount of formal schooling they have completed. Those characteristics influence the jobs they seek and the wages they earn.[7]

Differences in educational attainment—both between native-born and foreign-born workers and among the foreign-born workers themselves—are striking. Nearly all workers age 25 and older who were born in the United States have completed at least nine years of education, whereas 18 percent of foreign-born workers have completed eight or fewer years (see Table 4). Likewise, about 6 percent of native-born workers lacked a high school diploma or a GED compared with 29 percent of foreign-born workers.[8]

The high percentage of foreign-born workers without a diploma or a GED consists primarily of those from Mexico and Central America. Nearly 40 percent of them have completed fewer than nine years of education and another 20 percent have at least nine years but lack a high school diploma. As noted in Table 2, workers from Mexico and Central America have completed an average of about nine years of formal schooling compared with an average of about 14 years for those from the rest of the world and native workers. That five-year disparity is far greater than the disparities among major groups of native-born workers. For example, the largest difference

---

7. For a recent analysis of the effect of education on the earnings of immigrants, see George J. Borjas and Lawrence F. Katz, *The Evolution of the Mexican-Born Workforce in the United States*, Working Paper No. 11281 (Cambridge, Mass.: National Bureau of Economic Research, April 2005).

8. States award high school completion credentials to people who have not completed the requirements for a regular high school diploma but have passed the General Educational Development tests, or GED.

Table 4.

Educational Attainment of the U.S. Labor Force Age 25 and Older, by Nativity, 2004

(Percent)

	All Levels of Attainment	8th Grade or Less	9th to 12th Grade, No Diploma	High School Diploma or GED[a]	Some College or an Associate's Degree	Bachelor's Degree	Graduate Courses or Graduate Degree
				Distribution of Educational Attainment			
Total	100	4	6	30	28	21	11
Native Born	100	1	5	31	30	21	11
Foreign Born	100	18	11	25	16	18	12
Mexico and Central America	100	39	20	24	10	5	2
Rest of world	100	5	6	25	20	25	18
				Share of Educational Attainment Group			
Total	100	100	100	100	100	100	100
Native Born	85	28	73	88	91	87	84
Foreign Born	15	72	27	12	9	13	16
Mexico and Central America	6	58	18	4	2	1	1
Rest of world	10	14	9	8	7	12	15

Source: Congressional Budget Office based on the Bureau of the Census, Current Population Surveys, 2004.

a.   States award high school completion credentials to people who have not completed the requirements for a regular high school diploma but have passed the General Educational Development (GED) tests.

between groups of native-born workers classified by race and ethnic group is less than three years.

Thus, while immigrants represent only 15 percent of the total labor force, they account for over 70 percent of workers with no more than an eighth grade education and over 25 percent of workers with nine to 12 years of education but no high school diploma. Those shares have risen over the past decade, because of the influx of workers from Mexico and Central America with little education and because of a decline in the number of native-born workers who have not finished high school.

School enrollment rates among young immigrants suggest that those gaps in educational attainment are not likely to close in the near future. Among people ages 16 to 24, those born in Mexico or Central America are less than half as likely to be in school as natives or immigrants from other parts of the world (see Table 5). Furthermore, 60 percent of those immigrants from Mexico and Central America who are not enrolled in school have not finished high school compared with about 20 percent of natives and those from other parts of the world.

At the other end of the educational scale, immigrants from the rest of the world are much more likely to have taken graduate courses or obtained a graduate degree than are native-born workers or workers from Mexico and Central America (18 percent of immigrants from the rest of the world, compared with 11 percent of natives and 2 percent of immigrants from Mexico and Central America). Again, the marked difference in graduate education between immigrants from the rest of the world and those from Mexico and Central America probably reflects the difference in the basis for their entry into the United States. Workers with graduate education are much more likely to qualify for employment-based admission than are other workers.[9]

In addition to educational attainment, other characteristics of immigrants—their age, citizenship, and how long

9.   Over 80 percent of those whose admissions were based on an employment preference (and whose occupations are known) were in executive, managerial, professional, or technical occupations, which are generally associated with high levels of educational attainment. See Department of Homeland Security, *2003 Yearbook of Immigration Statistics*, p. 28.

Table 5.

Selected Characteristics of the U.S. Population and Labor Force, by Nativity, 2004

	Population Ages 16 to 24		Labor Force Age 25 and Older					
	Percentage Enrolled in School or College	Percentage of Not Enrolled That Are Not High School Graduates	Average Years of Education Completed	Average Age	Percentage That Are Male	Percentage That Are Citizens	Percentage That Came to Stay in U.S. at Age 15 or Younger	Percentage That Came to Stay in U.S. Before 1990
Total	56	24	13.7	44	54	91	n.a.	n.a.
Native Born	58	20	13.9	44	53	100	n.a.	n.a.
Foreign Born	44	46	12.3	41	60	43	21	54
Mexico and Central America	25	60	9.3	38	67	25	22	52
Rest of world	62	21	14.1	43	55	53	20	55

Source: Congressional Budget Office based on the Bureau of the Census, Current Population Surveys, 2004.

Note: n.a. = not applicable.

they have been in the United States, for example—may affect their role in the labor market. Workers from Mexico and Central America are about five years younger, on average, than native-born workers and workers from other parts of the world. However, their potential labor market experience (the number of years since completion of their schooling) may be about the same as a result of their lower level of formal educational attainment.

Workers from Mexico and Central America are less than half as likely as workers from other parts of the world to be naturalized citizens. Only a small part of that difference reflects the fact that more workers from Mexico and Central America have arrived recently. The difference is more likely to be a result of the higher share of unauthorized immigrants among people from Mexico and Central America. Their status as unauthorized immigrants is likely to reduce their labor market opportunities and produce poorer labor market outcomes. Alternatively, some workers born in Mexico and Central America may travel back and forth between their country of origin and the United States and find it difficult or unnecessary to pursue U.S. citizenship.

Foreign-born workers who have been in the United States for many years are likely to be well established in the U.S. labor market. In 2004, about half of foreign-born workers indicated that they came to the United States to stay before 1990. A substantial portion of foreign-born workers have lived in the United States since they were chil-

dren. Those workers are likely to have spent some time in the U.S. educational system and their entire working lives in the United States. About 20 percent of all foreign-born workers came to the United States to stay when they were 15 years old or younger.

Labor Market Outcomes

The labor market experience of immigrants differs from that of natives in three key ways: the likelihood of being employed, the type of work they do, and their compensation. Once again, those differences are much greater for immigrants from Mexico and Central America than they are for immigrants from the rest of the world.

Labor Force Participation, Employment, and Unemployment. In most age groups, a higher percentage of men from Mexico and Central America are in the labor force than are native-born men or other male immigrants (see Table 6). Despite their lower educational attainment, finding work does not appear to be a problem for men from Mexico and Central America. Their unemployment rate in 2004 (5.6 percent) was, in fact, similar to that of native-born men (5.7 percent). Male immigrants from the rest of the world had a somewhat higher labor force participation rate and a slightly lower unemployment rate than did native-born males.

Three factors may account for the higher participation rates of men from Mexico and Central America. First, young men who immigrated from that region are much

Table 6.

Labor Force Status of the Population Age 16 and Older, 2004

	Male			Female		
	Percentage in Labor Force	Percentage Employed	Unemployment Rate	Percentage in Labor Force	Percentage Employed	Unemployment Rate
Age 16 and Older						
Total	73.3	69.2	5.6	59.2	56.0	5.4
Native Born	72.0	67.9	5.7	60.0	56.9	5.3
Foreign Born	81.0	76.8	5.2	53.8	50.4	6.4
Mexico and Central America	87.9	83.0	5.6	50.7	46.3	8.6
Rest of world	76.3	72.6	4.8	55.3	52.4	5.4
Ages 16 to 24						
Total	63.6	55.5	12.6	58.7	52.3	11.0
Native Born	62.7	54.4	13.3	60.0	53.3	11.2
Foreign Born	70.0	63.9	8.7	47.8	43.7	8.6
Mexico and Central America	81.1	75.2	7.3	45.2	41.5	8.1
Rest of world	57.4	51.1	10.9	49.9	45.4	8.9
Ages 25 to 34						
Total	92.1	86.9	5.7	73.5	69.4	5.6
Native Born	92.0	86.5	6.0	77.0	72.8	5.4
Foreign Born	92.6	88.3	4.7	58.1	54.2	6.8
Mexico and Central America	95.5	90.5	5.2	50.1	45.3	9.5
Rest of world	89.5	85.8	4.1	64.4	61.1	5.1
Ages 35 to 44						
Total	91.9	88.1	4.1	75.7	72.2	4.5
Native Born	91.5	87.8	4.1	77.2	73.9	4.3
Foreign Born	93.7	89.6	4.4	68.2	64.1	6.1
Mexico and Central America	95.1	91.2	4.2	61.5	56.0	8.9
Rest of world	92.7	88.5	4.5	72.0	68.6	4.7
Ages 45 to 54						
Total	87.3	84.0	3.8	76.4	73.6	3.7
Native Born	86.9	83.6	3.7	77.3	74.7	3.4
Foreign Born	90.6	86.4	4.6	70.4	66.3	5.9
Mexico and Central America	90.2	84.5	6.3	64.2	59.5	7.3
Rest of world	90.8	87.3	3.8	72.8	68.9	5.4
Ages 55 to 64						
Total	68.9	66.2	3.9	56.5	54.4	3.7
Native Born	68.1	65.5	3.8	57.3	55.3	3.5
Foreign Born	75.3	71.4	5.2	50.6	47.5	6.0
Mexico and Central America	75.1	69.4	7.6	39.3	35.9	8.7
Rest of world	75.4	72.0	4.4	53.8	50.9	5.4
Age 65 and Older						
Total	18.8	18.1	3.6	11.1	10.7	3.0
Native Born	18.6	18.0	3.2	11.3	10.9	3.0
Foreign Born	20.3	19.0	6.5	9.5	9.3	2.9
Mexico and Central America	22.6	20.7	8.3	8.6	8.0	7.7
Rest of world	19.8	18.6	6.0	9.7	9.5	2.1

Source: Congressional Budget Office based on the Bureau of the Census, Current Population Surveys, 2004.

Figure 1.

Employment Status of the Population Ages 25 to 64, by Educational Attainment, 2004

(Percentage employed)

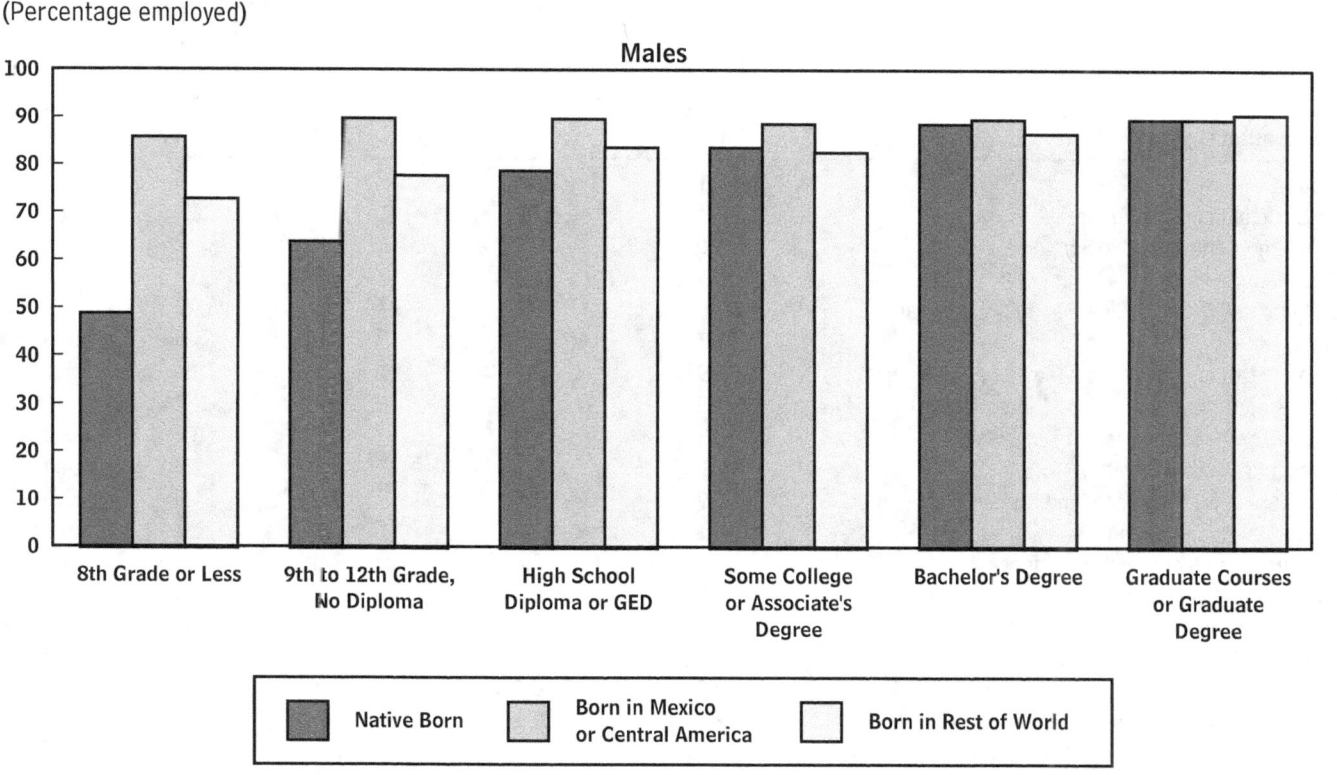

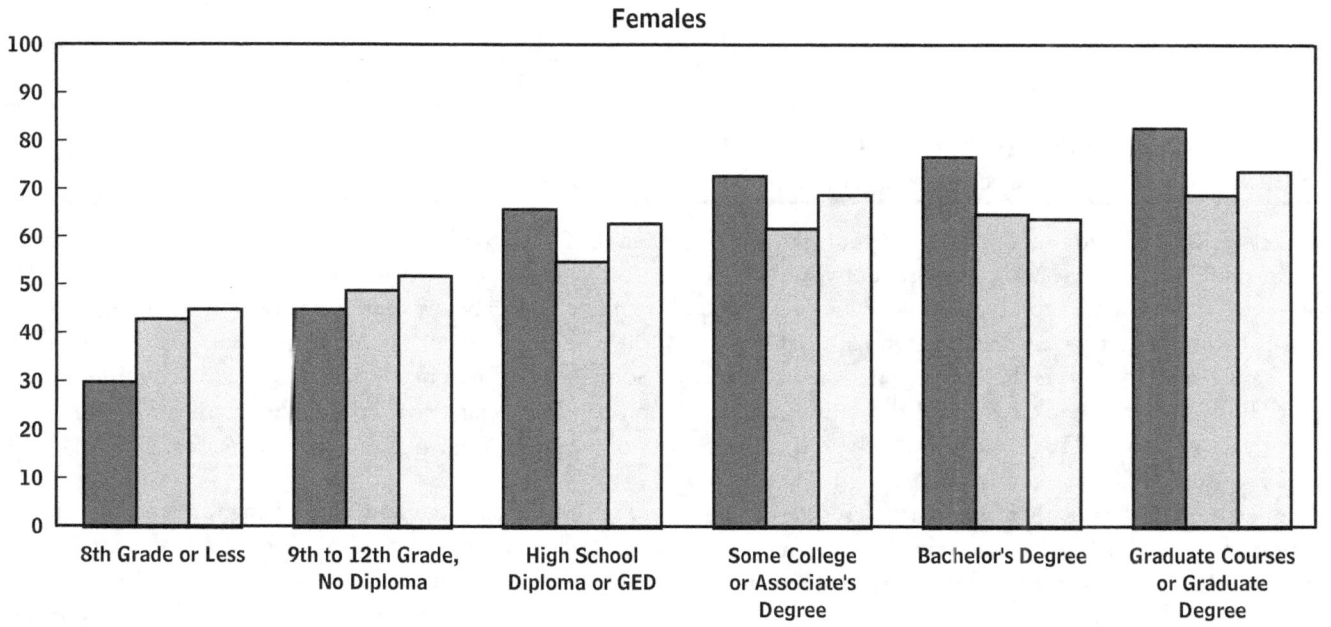

Source: Congressional Budget Office based on the Bureau of the Census, Current Population Survey, 2004.

Table 7.

Occupational Distribution of Workers Ages 25 to 64, by Nativity, 2004

(Percent)

Occupation Group	Total	Native-Born Workers	Foreign-Born Workers		
			Total	Mexico and Central America	Rest of World
Production	7.1	6.4	11.0	15.6	8.3
Construction and Extraction	6.1	5.6	9.2	17.3	4.4
Office and Administrative Support	13.6	14.5	8.9	6.2	10.5
Sales and Related	10.4	10.7	8.8	5.7	10.7
Building and Grounds Cleaning and Maintenance	3.6	2.8	8.4	15.0	4.5
Management	11.7	12.4	7.5	3.3	10.0
Transportation and Material Moving	5.9	5.7	6.9	10.0	5.1
Food Preparation and Serving Related	3.5	2.9	6.8	9.4	5.2
Health Care Practitioner and Technical	5.3	5.4	4.8	0.9	7.0
Personal Care and Service	2.9	2.8	3.7	2.5	4.4
Installation, Maintenance, and Repair	3.9	3.9	3.3	4.0	3.0
Education, Training, and Library	6.1	6.5	3.3	1.3	4.5
Computer and Mathematical Science	2.5	2.4	3.2	0.3	4.8
Business and Financial Operations	4.5	4.8	2.9	0.8	4.1
Health Care Support	2.0	1.9	2.5	1.2	3.4
Architecture and Engineering	2.2	2.2	2.1	0.3	3.2
Farming, Fishing, and Forestry	0.6	0.4	1.7	3.9	0.3
Arts, Design, Entertainment, Sports, and Media	2.0	2.1	1.4	0.7	1.8
Life, Physical, and Social Science	1.1	1.1	1.1	0.1	1.7
Protective Service	2.1	2.3	1.0	0.5	1.2
Community and Social Service	1.7	1.8	1.0	0.7	1.2
Legal	1.3	1.4	0.5	0.2	0.7
Total	**100.0**	**100.0**	**100.0**	**100.0**	**100.0**

Source: Congressional Budget Office based on the Bureau of the Census, Current Population Surveys, 2004.

Note: Occupation groups are ordered by the percentage of foreign-born workers employed in them.

less likely to be attending school than are young men born in the United States, and out-of-school youth are more likely than students to be working or looking for work. Second, many native-born men who are not in the labor force report in surveys that they are disabled or have retired. Foreign-born people who have disabilities that prevent them from working may be unlikely to immigrate to, or remain in, the United States. Third, because of financial constraints, early retirement is less likely to be an option for workers from Mexico and Central America. Moreover, those who do retire might choose to return to their country of origin.

The overall picture is quite different for foreign-born women, especially those from Mexico and Central Amer-

ica. In 2004, the labor force participation rate of women from Mexico and Central America was almost 10 percentage points below that of native-born women, and their unemployment rate was 3 percentage points higher. Some of the difference in labor force participation is probably associated with the higher fertility rates of women from Mexico and Central America.

Notably, the employment rates of the foreign born are not as closely associated with their educational attainment as are the employment rates of natives. In contrast to the case among native-born males, foreign-born males with less than a high school education are almost as likely to work as those with a bachelor's degree (see Figure 1 on page 11). Among foreign-born females, those with at

Table 8.

Distribution of Workers Ages 25 to 64 Across Occupations, by Education Level of Occupation, 2004

	Education Level of the Occupation Group				
	Very Low[a]	Low	Middle	High	Very High[a]
	Years of Education				
Average for Native-Born Workers in the Group	11.8	12.2	13.8	16.2	16.9
Range of the Averages for Native-Born Workers Across Occupations in the Group	10.5 to 12.0	10.5 to 12.7	12.7 to 15.0	15.0 to 18.0	16.0 to 18.0
	Percentage of Workers Employed in the Occupation Group				
	Both Sexes				
Native Born	6.7	25.9	47.9	26.2	12.8
Foreign Born					
Mexico and Central America	33.9	74.5	21.6	3.9	1.9
Rest of world	9.8	31.8	40.3	26.2	13.5
	Male				
Native Born	8.3	34.6	41.9	23.5	11.3
Foreign Born					
Mexico and Central America	30.1	80.1	17.2	2.6	1.3
Rest of world	9.5	34.9	37.3	27.8	14.4
	Female				
Native Born	4.9	16.2	54.6	29.1	14.5
Foreign Born					
Mexico and Central America	42.0	62.4	30.9	6.8	3.2
Rest of world	10.1	27.9	44.1	27.9	12.4

Source: Congressional Budget Office based on the Bureau of the Census, Current Population Surveys, 2004.

Notes: The occupations are ordered by the average years of school completed by native workers in the occupation.

Examples of occupations in which foreign-born workers are concentrated in relatively large numbers: Very Low—agricultural workers, dishwashers and cooks, maids, helpers on construction sites, hand packagers; Low—grounds maintenance workers, painters, contruction workers; Middle—food service managers; High—registered nurses, computer programmers, accountants and auditors; Very High—college teachers, physicians and surgeons, computer software engineers.

a. Very Low is a component of Low, and Very High is a component of High. The percentages for Low, Middle, and High add to 100.

least a high school diploma are much less likely to work than are those with a bachelor's degree, but the difference is smaller than it is for native-born females.

Type of Work. Almost half of all workers from Mexico and Central America are in three of 22 occupational groups: production; construction and extraction; and building and grounds cleaning and maintenance (see Table 7). Fewer than one in five native workers and workers from other parts of the world are in those occupations. Immigrant workers from other parts of the world have more broadly distributed occupations, although they are more likely than either natives or workers from Mexico and Central America to be in computer and

mathematical sciences; life, physical, and social sciences; and health care occupations.

Many workers who immigrated from Mexico and Central America are employed in occupations that require little formal education. When occupations are ranked according to the average educational level of native workers in those occupations, three-quarters of workers from Mexico and Central America—but only one-quarter of native workers—are in the relatively low-education occupations (see Table 8). Workers from Mexico and Central America fill large proportions of low-education jobs on construction sites and at restaurants, but very few are in the high-education occupations.

Table 9.

Distribution of Workers Ages 25 to 64 Across Major Industry Groups and Selected Subgroups, by Nativity, 2004

(Percent)

Major Industry Groups and Selected Subgroups	Total	Native-Born Workers	Foreign-Born Workers		
			Total	Mexico and Central America	Rest of World
Agriculture	1.3	1.2	1.8	4.2	0.4
Forestry, Logging, Fishing, Hunting	0.2	0.2	0.1	0.1	0.1
Mining	0.4	0.5	0.2	0.2	0.2
Construction	7.9	7.5	10.1	17.8	5.5
Manufacturing	12.9	12.5	14.8	17.9	12.9
Computer and electronic products	1.3	1.1	2.1	0.9	2.8
Furniture and fixtures manufacturing	0.5	0.5	0.6	1.1	0.4
Food manufacturing	1.2	1.0	2.2	4.2	1.0
Textile, apparel, and leather manufacturing	0.7	0.6	1.5	2.2	1.1
Wholesale Trade	3.5	3.5	3.3	3.6	3.2
Retail Trade	10.1	10.1	9.9	8.1	11.0
Transportation and Utilities	5.5	5.6	4.7	3.7	5.3
Information	2.6	2.8	1.5	0.6	2.1
Financial Activities	7.4	7.8	5.5	2.8	7.1
Professional and Business Services	10.5	10.3	11.7	11.8	11.7
Administrative and support services	3.7	3.3	6.1	9.7	4.0
Services to buildings and dwellings	0.9	0.7	2.1	3.4	1.3
Landscaping services	0.8	0.5	2.0	4.5	0.4
Education and Health Services	21.6	22.5	16.6	8.0	21.7
Leisure and Hospitality	6.3	5.4	10.9	13.1	9.6
Accommodations	1.0	0.8	2.3	2.5	2.1
Food services and drinking places	3.6	3.0	7.3	9.4	6.1
Other Services	4.8	4.5	6.8	7.3	6.5
Personal and laundry services	1.5	1.3	2.4	1.7	2.9
Private households	0.5	0.3	1.5	2.4	0.9
Public Administration	5.1	5.7	2.1	0.8	2.8
Total[a]	100.0	100.0	100.0	100.0	100.0

Source: Congressional Budget Office based on the Bureau of the Census, Current Population Surveys, 2004.

a. Percentages in the major industry groups sum to 100.

For workers from the remaining regions of the world, their distribution across occupations ranked by educational attainment is much like that of native workers except that they are somewhat less likely to be in the middle group of occupations. That pattern appears to reflect their educational distribution. Nevertheless, half of the workers from other parts of the world are in occupations where only about one-quarter of native workers are found. They are concentrated in some occupations that require little formal education, such as taxi drivers, and in

certain other occupations that require very high levels of education, such as college teachers.

Workers from Mexico and Central America are also heavily concentrated in certain industries (see Table 9). In 2004, about half of those workers ages 25 to 64 were employed in just eight sectors: construction (18 percent); restaurants (9 percent); landscaping (5 percent); agriculture (4 percent); food manufacturing (4 percent); services to buildings and dwellings (3 percent); textile, apparel, and leather manufacturing (2 percent); and private households (2 percent). Only about 15 percent of workers born in the United States and other parts of the world were employed in those industries. Workers who immigrated from other regions of the world were more broadly distributed across industries, just as they were across occupations.

Earnings. Foreign-born workers earn less than native workers, with lower educational attainment accounting for a major part of the difference. In 2004, the average weekly earnings of foreign-born men working full time were 78 percent of those of their native counterparts ($745 versus $959); the average weekly earnings of foreign-born women were 87 percent of those of native-born women ($625 versus $717). (See Table 10.)

Those differences can be directly linked to the lower earnings of workers from Mexico and Central America. The average earnings of men from Mexico and Central America were about half of those of native men, while the earnings of men from the rest of the world were virtually the same as those of native men. Likewise, the average earnings of women from Mexico and Central America were about 60 percent of those of native women, while those of other female immigrants were similar to those of native women.

In turn, much of the difference in the earnings of workers from Mexico and Central America can be linked to their lower educational attainment. For example, note in the lower section of Table 10 that the average earnings of men from Mexico and Central America within each educational category are at least 70 percent of those of native men with similar educational attainment.[10] The overall average of 54 percent is much lower than any of its components because those immigrants are disproportionately in the lower educational categories. Had full-time male workers from Mexico and Central America had the same educational distribution as natives, they would have earned 29 percent less than native men, rather than 46 percent less (see Table 11). Moreover, if they had also had as many potential years of experience as native men (based on their age and education), they would have

earned 27 percent less than native men.[11] Similar findings were estimated for women.

For full-time workers from other parts of the world, in contrast, accounting for education increases the earnings difference because those workers have somewhat higher levels of educational attainment than natives do. Adjusting for educational attainment, foreign-born men from the rest of the world earn 11 percent less than their native counterparts, but overall, they earn only 3 percent less because they have somewhat more education. Accounting for potential years of labor market experience has very little effect on the calculated wage differences because those foreign-born workers are about the same age as native workers. For women from other parts of the world, adjusting for their slightly higher educational attainment creates a small earnings gap.

That statistical analysis, however, has several limitations. In particular, the measures of educational attainment and labor market experience are imperfect. About one in five foreign-born workers came to the United States at an age when they were young enough to have attended U.S. schools.[12] The others, however, were either educated in their country of origin or received some education in the United States when they were older. In either case, the education that foreign-born workers receive may have a smaller effect on their earnings in U.S. labor markets than a U.S. education has for native workers.[13]

As in the case of education, labor market experience in an immigrant's country of origin is likely to be less valuable to U.S. employers than labor market experience in the United States; experience in the country of origin, moreover, may not be measured accurately. Some research suggests that labor market experience in an immigrant's

---

10. The specific comparisons reported in Tables 10 and 11 are with natives whose parents are also natives—that is, natives who are at least second-generation Americans. That was done because the next section of this paper compares the earnings of foreign-born workers with the earnings of workers from the second generation.

11. Although no direct measure of labor market experience is available, the years of potential labor market experience can be calculated. For example, assuming a high school student typically graduates at age 17, a 25-year-old high school graduate has a potential of eight years of labor market experience. That approximation is less accurate for women as a measure of actual experience because they are more likely to have spent time outside of the paid labor force.

12. Sherrie A. Koussoudji, "Immigrant Worker Assimilation: Is It a Labor Market Phenomenon?" *Journal of Human Resources,* vol. 24, no. 3 (1989).

13. Rachel M. Friedberg, "You Can't Take It with You? Immigrant Assimilation and the Portability of Human Capital," *Journal of Labor Economics,* University of Chicago, vol. 18, no. 2 (2000).

Table 10.

Average Weekly Earnings of Full-Time Workers Ages 25 to 64, by Educational Attainment, 2004

	All Levels of Attainment	8th Grade or Less	9th to 12th Grade, No Diploma	High School Diploma or GED[a]	Some College or Associate's Degree	Bachelor's Degree	Graduate Courses or Graduate Degree
	Average Weekly Earnings (Dollars)						
	Males						
Total	922	459	554	728	858	1,194	1,480
Native Born	959	545	583	749	871	1,217	1,496
Parents native	955	548	586	749	869	1,219	1,491
Parent from Mexico or Central America[b]	758	518	524	634	801	1,032	1,692
Parents from rest of world	1,091	*	568	799	938	1,216	1,539
Foreign Born	745	437	498	600	735	1,039	1,416
Mexico and Central America	511	427	488	539	638	862	*
Rest of world	930	500	526	650	774	1,060	1,439
	Females						
Total	705	340	391	542	641	894	1,105
Native Born	717	361	400	549	642	902	1,109
Parents native	712	360	402	549	640	896	1,105
Parent from Mexico or Central America[b]	637	342	344	515	631	1,004	1,028
Parents from rest of world	824	412	426	581	686	959	1,164
Foreign Born	625	334	363	484	623	844	1,079
Mexico and Central America	421	322	338	444	547	722	*
Rest of world	711	368	401	501	643	859	1,103
	Average Weekly Earnings of Workers as a Percentage of the Average Earnings of Native Workers with Native Parents						
	Males						
Born in Mexico or Central America	54	78	83	72	73	71	*
Parent from Mexico or Central America[b]	79	95	89	85	92	85	113
Born in Rest of World	97	91	90	87	89	87	97
Parents from Rest of World	114	*	97	107	108	100	103
	Females						
Born in Mexico or Central America	59	89	84	81	85	81	*
Parent from Mexico or Central America[b]	89	95	86	94	99	112	93
Born in Rest of World	100	102	100	91	100	96	100
Parents from Rest of World	116	114	106	106	107	107	105

Source: Congressional Budget Office based on the Bureau of the Census, Current Population Surveys, 2004.

Note: * = 2 percent or less of the nativity group had attained this level of education, and the standard error of the estimated percentage is greater than 5 percentage points.

a.   States award high school completion credentials to people who have not completed the requirements for a regular high school diploma but have passed the General Educational Development (GED) tests.

b.   Those with one parent from Mexico or Central America and one from another part of the world are classified as having a parent from Mexico or Central America.

Table 11.

Differences in Average Weekly Earnings Between Foreign- and Native-Born Full-Time Workers Ages 25 to 64, Adjusted for Educational Attainment and Experience, 2004

(Percentage difference from native workers with native parents)

	Males			Females		
	Unadjusted	Adjusted for Educational Attainment	Adjusted for Educational Attainment and Experience	Unadjusted	Adjusted for Educational Attainment	Adjusted for Educational Attainment and Experience
Foreign-Born Workers from Mexico and Central America	-46	-29	-27	-41	-22	-21
Native Workers with a Parent from Mexico or Central America[a]	-21	-8	-5	-11	0	2
Foreign-Born Workers from Rest of World	-3	-11	-10	0	-3	-3
Native Workers with Parents from Rest of World	14	4	6	16	7	8

Source: Congressional Budget Office based on the Bureau of the Census, Current Population Surveys, 2004.

Note: Average weekly earnings adjusted for educational attainment uses the average earnings within educational levels for the group but shifts the percentage in the educational level to the percentage for native workers with native parents. Educational attainment is based on six categories of education ranging from an eighth grade education or less to graduate education, as shown in Table 10. A similar procedure is used for the adjustment for experience. A person's experience is his or her age minus the normal age of labor market entry corresponding to the person's educational attainment. The age of labor market entry ranges from 16 years to 25 years across the range of education levels.

a.   Those with one parent from Mexico or Central America and one from another part of the world are classified as having a parent from Mexico or Central America.

country of origin has very little impact on earnings in the destination country.[14]

The length of time that immigrants have been in the United States also influences their earnings. Foreign-born workers who came to the United States many years ago generally earn more than those who arrived more recently. For example, among males employed full time, those from Mexico and Central America who came between 2000 and 2004 earned about $420 per week compared with $610 for those who arrived in 1983 or earlier (see Figure 2).

That pattern can be interpreted in several different ways.[15] First, it may indicate the speed with which immigrants assimilate into the U.S. economy. Assimilation can include learning how to negotiate the U.S. labor market or gaining experience or skills that are particularly impor-

---

14. Friedberg, "You Can't Take It with You?"

15. Potentially some of the difference in their weekly earnings might be due to the fact that recent immigrants are much younger, on average, than those who came earlier. Older workers usually have more labor market experience, which is generally associated with higher earnings. In this group, however, such an association is not evident. For example, recent arrivals ages 25 to 34 earned about the same, on average, as recent arrivals who were older, perhaps indicating that labor market experience in their home country was not rewarded in the U.S. labor market.

Figure 2.

Average Weekly Earnings of Full-Time, Foreign-Born Workers Ages 25 to 64 in 2004, by the Year They Came to the United States to Stay

(Dollars per week)

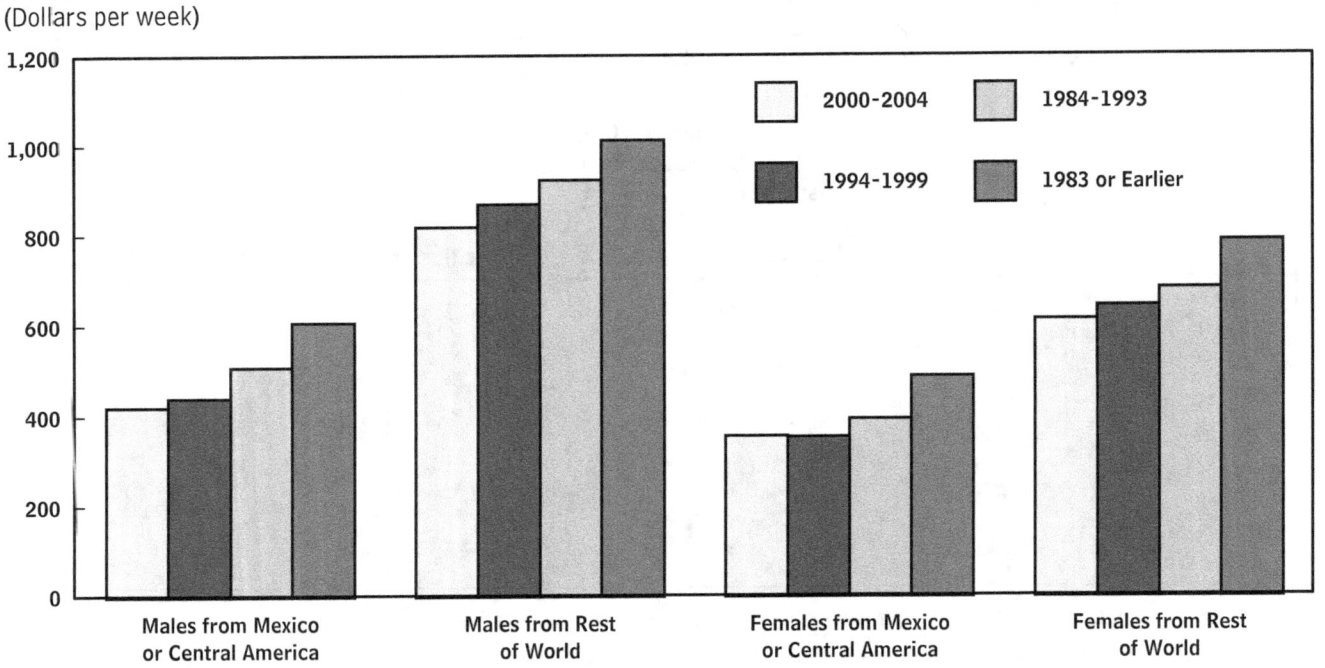

Source: Congressional Budget Office based on the Bureau of the Census, Current Population Survey, 2004.

tant in the United States, such as the ability to speak English.[16]

Second, it may be an indication of selective emigration— that is, those with poor labor market experiences in the United States may be more likely to return to their country of origin than those with better labor market experiences.[17]

Third, it may indicate that more-recent arrivals typically have fewer labor market skills that those who arrived previously, even within education and age groups. A 2005

study found that the earnings gap between recent immigrants from Mexico and native workers is increasingly due to the lower educational attainment of workers born in Mexico.[18]

The rate of assimilation might be dependent on a foreign-born worker's level of education. Some research finds that although the occupational gap between His-

---

16. Research indicates that English-language skill has a strong effect on earnings, with most of that effect associated with its impact on educational attainment. See Hoyt Bleakley and Aimee Chin, "Language Skills and Earnings: Evidence from Childhood Immigrants," *Review of Economics and Statistics,* vol. 86, no. 2 (2004), pp. 481-496. See also Sherrie A. Kossoudji, "English Language Ability and the Labor Market Opportunities of Hispanic and East Asian Immigrant Men," *Journal of Labor Economics,* University of Chicago. vol. 6, no. 2 (1988). The latter study finds that, at all levels of education, the economic cost of English-language deficiency is generally larger for Hispanic men than for Asian men.

17. Darren Lubotsky, *Chutes or Ladders? A Longitudinal Analysis of Immigrant Earnings,* Developmental Studies Paper 195 (Princeton, N.J.: Princeton University, Woodrow Wilson School of Public and International Affairs, August 2000). Lubotsky finds that immigrants' earnings grow 10 percent to 13 percent during their first 20 years in the United States relative to the earnings of natives with similar labor market experience. That is substantially less than the narrowing earnings gap observed for a particular cohort of immigrants from one decennial census to another. He suggests that emigration may account for the difference because he tracks the same group of individuals over time whereas the Census Bureau includes workers who later emigrate.

18. George J. Borjas and Lawrence F. Katz, *The Evolution of the Mexican-Born Workforce in the United States,* Working Paper No. 11281 (Cambridge, Mass.: National Bureau of Economic Research, April 2005).

Table 12.

Selected Characteristics of Workers Ages 25 to 64, by Nativity and Parents' Nativity, 2004

	Male				Female			
	Number (Thousands)	Average Years of Education Completed	Average Age	Average Years of Potential Labor Market Experience	Number (Thousands)	Average Years of Education Completed	Average Age	Average Years of Potential Labor Market Experience
All Workers	61,677	13.6	42	23	53,146	13.9	43	23
Native with Native Parents	47,607	13.9	43	23	43,097	14.1	43	23
Foreign Born from Mexico or Central America	4,400	9.2	38	20	2,054	9.9	39	22
Native with a Parent Born in Mexico or Central America[a]	843	12.8	37	19	701	13.0	38	19
Foreign Born from Rest of World	6,094	14.2	42	22	4,884	14.0	42	22
Native with Parents Born in Rest of World	2,733	14.8	42	22	2,411	14.8	42	22

Source: Congressional Budget Office based on the Bureau of the Census, Current Population Surveys, 2004.

a.   Those with one parent from Mexico or Central America and one from another part of the world are classified as having a parent from Mexico or Central America.

panic immigrants, non-Hispanic immigrants, and U.S.-born Hispanics narrows with the length of time spent in the United States, immigrants from Mexico with low levels of education start in low-status occupations, and their occupational status does not converge over time with that of non-Hispanic foreign-born workers or U.S.-born Hispanics.[19]

The Next Generation

Although foreign-born (first generation) workers are likely to earn substantially less than native workers during their working lives, the evidence suggests that the earnings gap is much smaller for their children (second generation), in large part due to their additional years of education, as well as to increases in earnings within educational groups. For example, adjusting for educational attainment and potential labor market experience, native-born men who had at least one parent from Mexico or Central America earned 5 percent less than other native-born men, while men from Mexico and Central America

earned 27 percent less (see Table 11 on page 17). The educational attainment of U.S.-born male children of immigrants from Mexico and Central America averaged 12.8 years of schooling compared with 9.2 years for male workers who were born in Mexico or Central America—a substantial improvement but still less than the 13.9 years of education that native-born men with native parents have received (see Table 12).

The Impact of Foreign-Born Workers on the U.S. Labor Market

Immigrants—especially immigrants with limited education—are often thought to be competing with certain native-born workers for low-skill jobs, thereby contributing to the widening earnings gap between high school dropouts and other workers. But some argue that many of those immigrants take jobs that would otherwise not exist or that complement the jobs of native workers, thereby increasing employment opportunities for natives. This section presents an analytic framework for considering how immigration can affect domestic labor markets and provides a critical review of the pertinent empirical literature.

---

19. Maude Toussaint-Comeau, *The Occupational Assimilation of Hispanics in the U.S.: Evidence from Panel Data*, Working Paper 2004-15 (Federal Reserve Bank of Chicago, 2004).

Analytic Framework

Foreign-born workers, who accounted for about 15 percent of all workers in 2004 and more than half of the growth of the workforce during the previous decade, hold a disproportionately large share of jobs that require very little education. Over one-third of all dishwashers, janitors, maids, and cooks are foreign born.

How would those jobs have been filled in the absence of the new immigrants? Presumably, some of those jobs would have been filled by other workers; in that case, employers might have been required to pay higher wages or to find other ways of making the jobs more attractive. Some jobs might not have been filled at all if employers were not ready to pay the required compensation; in that case, the goods and services would not have been produced. In other cases, employers might have changed the way that they produced those goods and services—for example, by automating or changing the mix of needed skills to better reflect those of the available labor pool.

Without new immigrant workers, some goods once produced in the United States might have been obtained through international trade. In the U.S. textile and apparel industry, for instance, one-third of the workers in 2004 were immigrants. In the absence of those foreign-born workers, the shift to trade-based sources might have been more rapid. Yet many immigrants, especially those with very low levels of education, were doing work—for example, washing dishes or cleaning hotel rooms—that cannot be done in another country. If the work they did was to be done at all, it had to be performed in the United States.

A simple supply-and-demand framework is useful for considering the potential effect of immigrants on employment opportunities for workers already in the United States. Suppose, for example, that one is trying to estimate the impact of a large number of immigrants with limited education on the wages and employment opportunities of U.S.-born high school dropouts. The initial effect is that the supply of unskilled labor increases. As a consequence, employers may be able to attract a sufficient number of workers without offering as high a wage as they would otherwise. The arrival of the immigrants leaves workers already in that market worse off because the jobs available to them pay less than they would have in the absence of the new workers. The affected workers can either work at the lower wage, search for a better job, or withdraw from the market. As costs of production are reduced, two outcomes are possible: the profits of employers increase and the prices that consumers pay for the products decrease. Either or both of these results may occur.

But that initial impact is likely to generate secondary changes in the supply of, and the demand for, labor as people adjust to the new situation. Those secondary changes, some perhaps occurring immediately and others developing over time, can mitigate the initial impact. On the supply side, for example, students who would face increased competition from immigrants if they dropped out of school might have an incentive to stay in school longer or find other ways to acquire skills that would better distinguish them from the immigrants. The consequent reduction in the supply of native high school dropouts would tend to raise wages in that market. At the same time, wages would also increase for workers who acquired the additional skills needed to lift themselves into a different, higher-wage market.

Likewise, the additional immigrants may induce greater demand because their presence either generates more demand for the product or attracts more capital. For example, the demand for labor might increase because the new immigrants purchase goods and services in that market or because new firms are attracted to the market by the availability of the additional workers.

The increase in the supply of one category of labor could affect demand or supply in other categories as well. The increased availability of registered nurses from abroad, for example, may make it more feasible for a hospital to expand its capacity, thereby increasing the demand for other hospital workers. Likewise, an expansion in the number of foreign-born child care workers could increase the number of native-born mothers of young children willing and able to work outside the home.

Although the supply-and-demand analytical framework is useful for identifying ways in which a labor market can adjust to an influx of immigrants, it does not, by itself, quantify those adjustments. Whether the presence of additional immigrants induces adjustments that ultimately result in higher or lower wages for different groups of workers is an empirical question. (See Box 2 for a discussion of how the growing presence of immigrants who earn below-average wages in itself lowers the growth in overall earnings.)

Box 2.

How an Increase in Foreign-Born Workers Can Affect Average Earnings Growth

Although the impact of an influx of foreign-born workers on the earnings of native-born workers is difficult to quantify, the presence of an increasing number of immigrant workers clearly reduces overall earnings growth. This occurs simply because foreign-born workers earn less than native workers, and that difference lowers the average earnings of the U.S. workforce as a whole.

Because a substantial share of foreign-born workers have not graduated from high school, their increased presence can also distort comparisons of trends in earnings by educational attainment. Thus, commonly cited statistics on earnings growth can be misleading if used as indicators of progress during a period in which an increasing share of the workforce is foreign born.

The growth in the average weekly earnings of men ages 25 to 64 working full-time during the past decade illustrates this point (see table below). Differences by educational attainment in the earnings growth of the entire group—that is, foreign- plus native-born men—follow a familiar pattern: the average earnings of men who had not graduated from high school rose by only about 2 percent, while that of college graduates increased by about 12 percent. However, the growth in the average earnings of native-born men within each educational category exceeded the growth in earnings for the corresponding foreign- plus native-born category. The earnings of native-born men (shown in the lower panel of the table) grew by about 2 percentage points more than the earnings of natives plus immigrants. Moreover, the differences in earnings growth between educational groups were much smaller for native-born men than for foreign- plus native-born men.

Average Weekly Earnings of Foreign- and Native-Born Men, by Educational Attainment, 1994 to 2004

	2004		1994 to 2004
	Number Employed (Thousands)	Average Weekly Earnings (Dollars)	Real Earnings Growth (Percentage Change)
Foreign- and Native-Born Men			
No Diploma	6,340	515	2.3
High School Diploma	17,690	730	4.3
Some College	15,035	860	6.2
Bachelor's Degree	19,240	1,290	11.9
Total	**58,300**	**920**	**10.1**
Native-Born Men			
No Diploma	3,160	575	5.4
High School Diploma	15,265	750	5.8
Some College	13,590	870	6.8
Bachelor's Degree	16,315	1,310	12.4
Total	**48,330**	**960**	**12.0**

Source: Congressional Budget Office based on the Bureau of the Census, Current Population Surveys, 1994 and 2004.

Note: Data are for full-time workers ages 25 to 64.

A Review of the Empirical Literature

A large number of studies have attempted to estimate the effects of immigration on native workers, but their conclusions reveal little consensus. The main challenge facing researchers has been to isolate the changes in labor market outcomes for native workers that are caused by the presence of foreign-born workers from the changes that would have occurred anyway. Unable to rerun economic history without immigration, researchers have used statistical techniques to try to isolate those effects. In doing so, most researchers have used one of two approaches: the area approach or the nationwide approach.

The Area Approach. Most of the studies have focused on areas where a large increase in the number of immigrants has occurred. That approach is based on the assumption that any initial adverse effects on native workers are most likely to show up in locations with particularly large inflows or concentrations of immigrants. The studies compare the experiences of native workers in areas with substantial increases in immigration with the experiences of native workers in areas that did not have such increases. The differences in those experiences, after statistically controlling for other factors, are then attributed to immigration.

A review of those studies in the mid-1990s, conducted as part of an examination of immigration by the National Research Council, found that the studies "show only a weak relationship between native wages and the number of immigrants in a city or state. Furthermore, in these studies the numerically weak relationship between native wages and immigration is observed across all types of native workers, skilled and unskilled, male and female, minority and nonminority. The one group that appears to suffer substantially from new waves of immigration are immigrants from earlier waves, for whom the recent immigrants are close substitutes in the labor market."[20]

One frequently cited study based on the area approach is an analysis of the labor market in Miami after the sudden arrival of a large number of Cuban immigrants—the Mariel immigrants—in 1980. The author of the study, David Card, estimated that the influx of immigrants had virtually no effect on the wages of workers already in that labor market, even though it increased the size of the Miami labor force by 7 percent in less than one year.[21] He attributed the ability of the Miami labor market to adjust to such a large influx of new immigrants to two characteristics of that market. First, because of previous waves of immigration, Miami already had a large number of employers (especially apparel and textile firms) that were able to expand their operations to absorb the new immigrants. Second, the arrival of the new immigrants might have dissuaded other workers from moving to Miami, which was already a popular destination for people from other countries and other parts of the United States.[22]

More recent studies based on differences across a large number of local labor markets have continued to find little, if any, adverse effect on native workers. For example, based on his analysis of data from the 2000 census for about 300 metropolitan areas, David Card concluded, "Although immigration has a strong effect on relative supplies of different skill groups, local labor market outcomes of low skilled natives are not much affected by these relative supply shocks."[23]

Researchers disagree about how to interpret the results from studies based on differences in labor market outcomes across locations. Taken at face value, the results suggest that the addition of large numbers of foreign-born workers to a labor market has little or no impact on

20. James P. Smith and Barry Edmonston, eds., *The New Americans: Economic, Demographic, and Fiscal Effects of Immigration* (Washington, D.C.: National Academy Press, 1997), p. 6. A recent statistical analysis of about 350 estimates of immigration's impact on wages, drawn from studies conducted in the United States, Europe, Israel, and Australia, also found that most of the estimated impacts were small. Over two-thirds of the estimates were based on the area approach. See Simonetta Longhi, Peter Nijkamp, and Jacques Poot, "A Meta-Analytic Assessment of the Effect of Immigration on Wages," *Journal of Economic Surveys*, vol. 19, no. 3 (2005), pp. 451-477.

21. David Card, "The Impact of the Mariel Boatlift on the Miami Labor Market," *Industrial and Labor Relations Review*, vol. 43, no. 2 (1990), pp. 245-257.

22. A recent analysis of production processes in Miami suggests a third explanation: firms there might have slowed their introduction of labor-saving machinery in response to the influx of a large number of unskilled workers. See Ethan Lewis, *How Did the Miami Labor Market Absorb the Mariel Immigrants?* Working Paper 04-3 (Federal Reserve Bank of Philadelphia, 2004).

23. David Card, *Is the New Immigration Really So Bad?* Working Paper No. 11547 (Cambridge, Mass.: National Bureau of Economic Research, August 2005), p. 24.

the earnings of workers already there.[24] But critics of that approach point out that the location decisions of foreign-born workers are likely to be influenced by potential wages. Thus, the failure to find a significant effect may simply mean that immigrants tend to move to places where the job opportunities are best. Had the foreign-born workers not arrived, the workers already present might have gained more from the strong labor market.

Moreover, an influx of foreign-born workers could trigger the movement of employers to that location and the movement of other workers out of it. To the extent that employers or workers adjust their location decisions in ways that offset the otherwise adverse impact of immigration, the effects will be diffused.

The considerable mobility of the population provides support for such potential adjustments. For example, data from the 2000 census indicate that about 8 percent of the respondents were living in a different state than they had been five years earlier, and 10 percent were living in a different county within the same state. Moreover, 18 percent of the foreign-born population had been living outside the United States five years earlier.[25] To the extent that the decisions of those movers were influenced by the availability of job opportunities and the wages associated with those jobs, the estimated impacts on earnings of an increased number of immigrants in specific locations could have understated the overall effects. The actual impact of labor market conditions on the migration decisions of foreign- and native-born workers, however, remains uncertain.

The Nationwide Approach. To overcome potential problems associated with estimating movements across areas, other studies have been based on nationwide variations in the number of immigrants over time. Those studies have used national data to examine changes in the earnings of different groups of native workers—categorized by educational attainment, work experience, or occupation—that are associated with changes in the number of immigrants with similar characteristics. That approach is based on the idea that the adverse effects of an influx of immigrants are most likely to show up among the workers whose employment-related characteristics are most similar to those of the immigrants. By using nationwide data, the approach does not miss effects from geographic adjustments by workers and employers. If, for example, the movement of Mexican high school dropouts into San Diego caused native high school dropouts to move to another U.S. city, national data could capture impacts that would be missed by looking only at data for San Diego.

A widely cited study by George Borjas illustrates this approach.[26] The author used data that the Census Bureau collected in its decennial census from 1960 through 2000 to classify male workers ages 18 to 64 by skill group. Having observed that employers are more likely to view workers with the same level of education as substitutes for one another if they have similar amounts of experience, Borjas defined a skill group in terms of both educational attainment and potential labor market experience, rather than educational attainment alone. Borjas found substantial variation in immigrants' share of employment in those education-experience categories over the 1960-2000 period. Those findings enabled him to estimate impacts on the average weekly earnings of 32 groups of men, from high school dropouts with less than six years of potential work experience to college graduates with over 35 years of experience.

That study estimated that a 10 percent increase in the number of workers in an education-experience category would reduce the average weekly earnings of men in that group by about 4 percent before secondary adjustments in capital formation or investments in skills by workers are made. Using a simulation of the impact of large numbers of immigrants analogous to the change in the number of foreign-born male workers between 1980 and 2000, Borjas calculated that the average weekly earnings of native-born men as a group would be reduced by 3 percent to 4 percent, with high school dropouts experiencing the largest adverse impact. He estimated that their

---

24. At least in the short run, an influx of foreign-born workers can increase the rental prices of local housing, thereby reducing the purchasing power of local workers who rent, even if their nominal wages are not affected. See Albert Saiz, "Room in the Kitchen for the Melting Pot: Immigration and Rental Prices," *Review of Economics and Statistics*, vol. 85, no. 3 (2003), pp. 502-521.

25. Marc J. Perry and Jason P. Schachter, *Migration of Natives and the Foreign Born: 1995 to 2000*, Census 2000 Special Reports (Bureau of the Census, August 2003), p. 3, available at www.census.gov/prod/2003pubs/censr-11.pdf.

26. George J. Borjas, "The Labor Demand Curve *Is* Downward Sloping: Reexamining the Impact of Immigration on the Labor Market," *Quarterly Journal of Economics*, vol. 18, no. 4 (2003), pp. 1335-1374.

earnings would be about 9 percent lower than they would be in the absence of increased competition from foreign-born workers.[27]

Although the use of national data should overcome the main problems with the area approach, the nationwide approach also has limitations. In particular, it does not account for the secondary adjustments that are likely to be made. As a result, it overstates the long-run impact of immigration on native workers' earnings if the presence of foreign-born workers stimulates the demand for workers—by attracting more capital, for example—or leads natives to acquire more education. Both adjustments to the presence of more foreign-born workers are likely to occur.

Borjas himself noted the potential importance of such adjustments in a recent paper that estimated the long-run impact of immigration on the earnings of native workers if the nation's capital stock increased by enough to keep the returns on capital constant. If complete adjustment of the capital stock occurred, Borjas found, there would be no long-run impact on the average weekly earnings of native men overall. In that situation, some groups would gain and other groups would lose; the workers most likely to lose would be those whose education and experience most closely resembled those of the new immigrants. In particular, Borjas estimated that the earnings of men without a high school diploma would be reduced by the influx of immigrants, although that long-run impact (-4 percent) was about half the size of the short-term impact.[28] Whether the nation's capital stock would adjust to the expansion of the immigrant workforce to the extent used in that illustration is not known, but it is certainly reasonable to assume that considerable adjustment would occur.[29]

Likewise, it is reasonable to assume that some natives would stay in school longer as a consequence of the influx of so many foreign-born workers who lack a high school education. Attaining a diploma is one way of moving into a different labor market. How much of the increase in educational attainment of the native population can be attributed to that cause is not known. But to the extent that it occurred, Borjas's original estimate would overstate the long-run impact of immigration on native workers' earnings.

Finally, foreign-born workers are employed disproportionately in some occupations, such as computer software engineers and physicians, which require a very high level of skill. Just as the addition of large numbers of foreign-born workers with less than a high school education could depress the earnings of native high school dropouts, so too the addition of large numbers of highly educated foreign-born workers could depress the earnings of highly educated native workers.

Again, the empirical literature has not agreed on a conclusion. One recent working paper estimated that the growth in the number of foreign-born recipients of U.S. doctoral degrees who planned to remain in the United States reduced the earnings of other workers who received doctoral degrees in the same field of study.[30] But another working paper estimated that an increase in the foreign-born percentage of workers in an occupation did not appear to reduce the earnings of native workers in skilled occupations, although it did have an adverse impact on workers in manual labor occupations.[31] Likewise, a study of the surge in skilled immigrants from the Soviet Union to Israel in the early 1990s found no adverse impact on the earnings of native workers with similar skills.[32]

27. Subsequently, Borjas made refinements in his analysis that resulted in slightly different estimates but did not change the basic findings.

28. George J. Borjas, *Wage Trends Among Disadvantaged Minorities*, NPC Working Paper No. 05-12 (Ann Arbor, Mich.: University of Michigan, National Poverty Center, August 2005).

29. In a different context, a recent analysis of adjustment costs, based on responses to variations in military spending and oil price shocks, suggests that capital can adjust quickly. See Robert E. Hall, "Measuring Factor Adjustment Costs," *Quarterly Journal of Economics*, vol. 119, no. 3 (2004), pp. 899-927.

30. George J. Borjas, *The Labor Market Impact of High-Skill Immigration*, Working Paper No. 11217 (Cambridge, Mass.: National Bureau of Economic Research, March 2005).

31. See Pia M. Orrenius and Madeline Zavodny, *Does Immigration Affect Wages? A Look at Occupation-Level Evidence*, Research Department Working Paper 0302 (Federal Reserve Bank of Dallas, August 2003).

32. Rachel M. Friedberg, "The Impact of Mass Migration on the Israeli Labor Market," *Quarterly Journal of Economics*, vol. 116, no. 4 (2001), pp. 1373-1408.

Implications for the Future as the Baby Boomers Exit the Labor Force

A significant, long-lasting shift in the age profile of the U.S. population is under way. The Census Bureau projects that between 2000 and 2050 the number of people age 65 and older will more than double, while the number of adults under age 65 will grow by about 35 percent.[33] That shift reflects demographic trends that have been in play for many years and are expected to continue into the future: the aging of the baby-boom generation (those born between 1946 and 1964) and the continued increases in life expectancy.

Beginning in the mid-1960s, members of the baby-boom generation poured into the labor force. Many baby boomers are now in their 50s and will soon become eligible for Social Security retirement benefits. Some of them have already withdrawn from the labor force, often because of a disability.[34]

The Congressional Budget Office (CBO) projects that total labor force growth over the next decade will be considerably slower than its historical rate of about 1.5 percent a year during the past half century. The slower projected pace stems from CBO's expectation that the percentage of the population that will be in the labor force will decline sharply during the next 10 years as the leading edge of the baby-boom generation reaches the traditional retirement age. It will also be spurred by other factors: the labor force participation rate of men is likely to continue its historical downward trend, and the participation rate of women is not expected to increase as much as it has in the past.[35]

The baby-boom generation's exit from the labor force could well foreshadow a major shift in the role of foreign-born workers in the labor force. Unless native fertility rates increase, it is likely that most of the growth in the U.S. labor force will come from immigration by the middle of the century. As long as people continue to move to and remain in the United States to work, the foreign-born share of the labor force will continue to grow.

Projections of immigration and other demographic variables are based on assumptions that are subject to considerable debate, but the likelihood that immigrants will continue to play a large and growing role in the U.S. labor market is very high. Census Bureau projections prior to the 2000 census illustrate the potential importance of immigration.[36] For its middle series, the Census Bureau's staff assumed that net migration to the United States would average roughly 900,000 to 1 million per year through 2050. Based on that and other assumptions, they projected that the total U.S. population would increase by about 128 million people between 2000 and 2050. In the absence of any immigration or emigration during that 50-year period, the increase would be only about 54 million people.[37] Put another way, about 60 percent of the projected population growth would come from new immigrants and their offspring.

More important, nearly all of the projected additions to the population associated with immigration are under age 65. Looking only at people ages 15 to 64, about 50 million—83 percent—of the projected 60 million increase in population in that age group would consist of new immigrants and their children. Therefore, future labor force growth is likely to be largely the result of immigration.

Thus, decisions regarding immigration policy—in particular, how many immigrants to admit, the criteria for entry, and how to deal with unauthorized admissions—

---

33. See Bureau of the Census, "Projected Population of the United States, by Age and Sex: 2000 to 2050," Internet release on March 18, 2004, available at www.census.gov/ipc/www/usinterimproj/natprojtab02a.pdf .

34. Congressional Budget Office, *Disability and Retirement: The Early Exit of Baby Boomers from the Labor Force* (November 2004).

35. The Congressional Budget Office's (CBO's) projections of potential labor force growth over the next decade are presented in *The Budget and Economic Outlook: An Update* (August 2005). CBO projects a 0.8 percent annual rate of growth in the size of the labor force, adjusted for cyclical variations. That is half the annual growth rate for the 1950 to 2004 period.

36. The Census Bureau subsequently released a new estimate of the size of the population in 2000 and new interim projections of population growth but not the detailed information needed to replicate the analysis reported in this paragraph. The Bureau's latest projections call for the total population to increase from about 280 million in 2000 to 420 million in 2050. See Bureau of the Census, "Projected Population of the United States."

37. Frederick W. Hollmann, Tammany J. Mulder, and Jeffrey E. Kallan, *Methodology and Assumptions for the Population Projections of the United States: 1999 to 2100*, Population Division Working Paper No. 38 (Bureau of the Census, Population Division, January 13, 2000). In subsequent methodological revisions, the Census Bureau increased the projected number of immigrants by about 10 percent, raising the portion of total population growth attributable to immigration.

are likely to shape the size and composition of the U.S. labor force well into the future.

If the new immigrants resemble those who arrived in recent years, they will enter the U.S. labor market with fewer years of education, on average, than native-born workers have and will be disproportionately employed in lower-skill occupations. Whether the retirement of the baby boomers and the growing demand for a wide range of services associated with an aging population will increase the relative earnings in such occupations is unknown.

The long-term impact of immigration on the size and composition of the U.S. labor force will also include the increased supply of labor that the immigrants' offspring provide. Children born in the United States to parents from Mexico and Central America are much more likely than the immigrants who were born there to have completed high school. As a result, their work-related characteristics are likely to more closely resemble those of other native-born workers.